ACHIEVE IT NOW

****

BEAT PROCRASTINATION FOR A BRIGHTER TOMORROW

****

MASTER YOUR TIME,
ACHIEVE YOUR DREAMS,
TRANSFORM YOUR LIFE,
UNLEASH THE POWER WITHIN YOU.

DILIP PATIL

www.patildilip.com

DEDICATION

I dedicate this book to my family, whose unwavering support and love have been the bedrock of my journey. You have constantly inspired and encouraged me to reach for the stars and believe in my potential. Your belief in me has given me the strength to persevere during the darkest moments and strive for greatness. This book is a testament to our shared values and the power of unity. May it serve as a reminder that ordinary lives can be transformed by cultivating success habits. Thank you for always being by my side and my greatest champion.

HEARTFELT GRATITUDE!

"In gratitude for your support and commitment to personal growth."

Dear Esteemed Reader,

I sincerely appreciate choosing 'Achieve It Now: Beat Procrastination for a Brighter Tomorrow.' Your trust and engagement in this journey are genuinely valued. As a token of gratitude, I am delighted to offer you an exclusive free e-book, "The Success Formula: Achieve Personal Growth, Excel Professionally, Unlock Your Potential, Transform Your Life." Click the link or scan the QR code below to download your gift.

Your support drives the 'Procrastination Triumph Series,' I hope this e-book contributes to your ongoing growth journey.

Thank you once again for being an integral part of this transformative community.

Warm regards,

Dilip Patil

Author, 'Achieve It Now: Beat Procrastination for a Brighter Tomorrow

TABLE OF CONTENTS

PREFACE

"The best way to get something done is to begin." —
Author Unknown.

Welcome to "Achieve It Now: Beat Procrastination for a Brighter Tomorrow," the inaugural installment in the "Procrastination Triumph Series." This quote encapsulates the essence of the journey we're about to embark upon—from procrastination to proactive transformation.

This book holds a deeply personal significance for me. It's born from my odyssey through the labyrinth of procrastination—both in my personal and professional life. I have encountered the lingering effects of delay, the missed opportunities, and the thwarted aspirations that procrastination can wield.

I have navigated the tumultuous seas of missed deadlines, hesitations, and the detours that delayed decisions often create. But it was through these struggles that I unearthed the invaluable keys to overcoming procrastination, which I now share with you through this series.

The genesis of this series stems from my profound belief that conquering procrastination is not just a matter of ticking tasks off a list. It's about charting a course to a brighter future—a future brimming with accomplishments and realized dreams.

Each book in this series is meticulously designed to serve as a compass, guiding you through a transformative journey from procrastination's clutches to personal mastery and fulfillment.

As you delve into the following pages, rest assured you're not alone in this expedition. We are in this together. I will share strategies and tactics to defeat procrastination and real-life examples and anecdotes illustrating the triumphs over delays in my life.

I implore you to engage with the material actively, reflect on your experiences with procrastination, and utilize the resources embedded within this series for an interactive and transformative experience.

My sincere gratitude extends to those who have inspired and bolstered the creation of this series. Additionally, I draw wisdom from countless individuals, researchers, and experts whose work has profoundly shaped my understanding of procrastination.

I invite you to anticipate practical strategies, valuable insights, and a procrastination-free future. Start this journey from procrastination to self-mastery.

To a Brighter Tomorrow,

DILIP PATIL

Author, "Procrastination Triumph Series"

INTRODUCTION

Confronting Procrastination's Grip

"Procrastination operates as the unseen pilferer of our time, the underminer of our grandest dreams, and the saboteur of our most cherished triumphs. Yet within each of us lies an antidote—a potency that permits us to seize the present and carve a destiny radiant with promise."

These resonant words echo the eternal struggle against the enigmatic clasp of procrastination. "Achieve It Now: Beat Procrastination for a Brighter Tomorrow" is the cornerstone of the "Procrastination Triumph" series—a guidebook meticulously etched from personal battles and resounding victories in the war against procrastination.

I am Dilip Patil, born in a modest village in the Wardha district of Maharashtra, India. My hardworking and humble parents lived in a mud-made house, navigating the challenges of daily wage labor. Fortune smiled upon us when my father secured a permanent job in a government organization a year after my birth. Despite his lack of formal education, he began as a laborer and soon got transferred to the city.

Driven by a genuine desire to provide a better future, my parents insisted on prioritizing education. They enrolled me in a Hindi medium school to ensure I wouldn't face the same hardships they encountered. However, financial strains persisted. In the sixth grade, I decided to work part-time, supporting my parents by assisting in a local grocery store owned by our landlord.

Balancing school and work proved challenging, but determination fueled my efforts. By the eighth grade, I faced a setback when I failed a subject due to procrastination stemming from the heavy workload. This failure became a crucial lesson, a turning point in my life. It marked the day I resolved never to procrastinate again, realizing its adverse impact.

With renewed focus, I managed both academic studies and my part-time job, eventually excelling in the 11th grade and securing admission to an engineering program. This journey, shaped by the consequences of procrastination, inspired me to share my experiences. Thus, the Procrastination Triumph Series was born, with "Achieve It Now: Beat Procrastination for a Brighter Tomorrow" as its inaugural book. Through my story, I aim to empower you to overcome procrastination and thrive personally and professionally.

I, the architect behind these pages, once found myself trapped in the entangling web of procrastination. It formed a seemingly inescapable labyrinth, constricting my ambitions and gnawing at the fabric of my aspirations.

Through an ardent and aggressive engagement, armed with tactics derived from personal encounters, I embarked on a journey to unravel and master its enigmatic ways.

Allow me to share a glimpse of this expedition. Envision a meticulously planned project, an embodiment of enthusiasm and aspirations. Yet, as the deadline loomed, I succumbed to the seductive allure of distractions, enveloping my progress in a shroud of delay. Procrastination's cunning promises of a vague "tomorrow" constructed an illusory sanctuary amidst the echoes of urgency.

In the throes of navigating this labyrinth with procrastination, a poignant moment stands out—a microcosm of the daily struggles that countless individuals encounter. It was within the genuine creation of what I deemed a masterpiece, a written testament to my passions. Each day, the allure of procrastination silently swirled around, weaving a deceptive cloak of comfort over the pressing need for action.

This battle against time, disguised in the subtle deceit of postponing endeavors for an indefinite future, unveiled a profound realization. In quiet moments of reflection, the echo of my struggle reverberated in the lives of many. The habitual deferral, the allure of comfortable delay, and the gradual erosion of ambitions beneath the guise of **"I will do it later"** manifested a profound revelation of how this seemingly innocuous habit had stealthily shaped choices and dictated the rhythm of progress in my life.

This personal chronicle mirrors the everyday skirmishes against procrastination, a struggle that transcends boundaries of profession, age, or background, intricately woven into the fabric of our lives, often imperceptible until its weight is felt. Through these shared experiences, I have unearthed an arsenal of strategies, culminating in the journey chronicled in this series—a voyage to emancipate us all from the shackles of procrastination.

A repository of methodologies and strategies emerged through unyielding self-examination and relentless research. From the structured bursts of productivity with the Pomodoro Technique to the serene mastery of mindfulness, these techniques stand as the bedrock of this series—a comprehensive arsenal against procrastination.

The expedition commences by dissecting the complex Procrastination Puzzle, revealing this habit beyond mere delay, unveiling its profound impacts on personal and professional spheres while dispelling prevailing misconceptions. Delving deeper, we'll explore the tangible and intangible costs, weaving real-life stories to illuminate the aftermath of deferred actions, igniting motivation to confront these unseen prices.

Venturing further, we'll delve into The Anatomy of Procrastination, uncovering the emotional triggers and thought patterns that fuel this habit. Transitioning towards actionable solutions, we'll navigate The Decision to Change, offering practical strategies and exercises marking the initial steps toward transformation.

The narrative progresses, constructing proactive habits, nurturing productivity through routines, and guiding you toward goal achievement. Identifying and managing triggers becomes pivotal in overcoming procrastination triggers, nurturing resilience amidst challenges, and paving the path toward resilience, rich with stories and exercises fortifying personal fortitude.

A vivid canvas will depict A Procrastination-Free Future, showing the liberating benefits of a procrastination-free life. You will be encouraged to envision and pursue this better future. This series celebrates theories, personal successes, setbacks, and strategy evolution in the face of adversity.

Join me on this transformative odyssey. Together, let's decipher the intricate riddles of procrastination, forging a future teeming with realized ambitions and boundless potential.

1 THE PROCRASTINATION PUZZLE

"The most effective way to do it is to do it." - Amelia Earhart.

Amelia Earhart's words echo a fundamental truth often obscured by the veils of procrastination. The subtle dance between productivity and delay has been a battleground I have traversed personally, a journey marked by the complex interplay of ambition and the silent assailant—procrastination. This habit, defined as the deferment of actions or tasks to a future time, transcends mere postponement; it infiltrates the essence of productivity and achievement, casting its shadow over personal and professional realms.

In the tapestry of my life, procrastination emerged as more than a delay tactic—it evolved into an intricate puzzle. Its impact reverberated through the corridors of personal ambition, eroding the vitality of dreams with the insidious allure of **'later.'** Professionally, its presence was a double-edged sword, disguising itself as mere time management while stealthily sabotaging the quality and timeliness of my work. What appeared as a postponement became a habitual deferment, veiling the urgency of the present moment and corroding the grandeur of aspirations.

This habit, seemingly innocuous in its inception, gradually metamorphosed into a sly saboteur, chipping away at the foundation of achievements. Its impact on personal life meant more than delayed tasks—it introduced a pervasive sense of unease, a constant undercurrent of unfulfilled potential that whispered discontent in moments of reflection.

Professionally, the impact was equally insidious. The guise of managing time cleverly camouflaged the dilution of quality, the compromise of standards, and the sly erosion of deadlines. It wasn't merely a matter of unfinished tasks; it became a silent erosion of credibility, an undercurrent of unmet promises, and a subtle tarnishing of professional reputation.

As I understood, the Procrastination Puzzle wasn't just about delaying tasks. It was a multifaceted web, interwoven with the intricate threads of habit, comfort, and a deceptive promise of **'later.'** It cast a shadow on the potential of what could be, obscuring the brilliance of achievement in a cloak of deferred action.

This chapter seeks to unfurl the enigma of procrastination, to define its complexity, and to explore its impact on personal and professional spheres. Through this exploration, we'll dissect this puzzle, peeling away the layers to reveal its multifaceted influence and pave the way toward dismantling the delay problem and unlocking the gates to productive fulfillment.

1.1 MYTH AND REALITY

Procrastination, often draped in misconceptions, presents a labyrinth of illusions and challenges. One of the prevalent fallacies is the belief that it merely entails postponing tasks. However, this habit goes beyond mere delay, infiltrating our psyche and influencing the quality and timeliness of our endeavors. The first challenge is recognizing that procrastination isn't solely about time management but a complex interplay of psychological, emotional, and habitual factors.

Another common misconception is the perceived correlation between procrastination and laziness. This erroneous assumption overlooks the nuanced psychological dynamics at play. Procrastination isn't a lack of willpower but is often a product of intricate emotional triggers, fear of failure, or overwhelming stressors. This misinterpretation further compounds individuals' challenges, leading to self-criticism and a downward spiral of decreased motivation.

The next challenge arises from the deceptive allure of immediate gratification. Procrastination sometimes arises from the preference for short-term relief over long-term gain. The quick fix of engaging in more immediately rewarding activities can lull individuals into a false sense of productivity while the pressing, significant tasks remain unattended.

Perfectionism, paradoxically, serves as both a misconception and a challenge within the realm of procrastination. While a quest for perfection can be commendable, it often becomes a disguised form of procrastination. The perpetual pursuit of flawless outcomes can paralyze progress, leading individuals to postpone tasks indefinitely, fearing not meeting their self-imposed standards.

In the professional sphere, the misconception of multitasking as an effective counter to procrastination presents a substantial challenge. Multitasking, presumed to enhance productivity, can instead fragment focus, leading to a dispersion of effort across various tasks without substantial progress on any.

Moreover, societal misconceptions around the nature of productivity exacerbate the challenges of procrastination. The notion that busyness equates to productivity perpetuates the false belief that constant activity signifies progress, sometimes fostering a deceptive comfort in constant motion without significant advancement.

These interconnected misconceptions and challenges make procrastination devastating to personal and professional life. Recognizing and dispelling these myths is the first step to understanding procrastination.

1.2 EMBRACE IMMEDIATE ACTION

Central to overcoming the intricate web of procrastination is the "Achieve It Now" concept, a proactive solution to reshape our approach to task execution. This methodology revolves around the philosophy of immediate action in the face of pending tasks, bypassing the snares of delay and excuses.

The essence of "Achieve It Now" lies in seizing the present moment, fostering a mindset of immediate initiation rather than postponement. It advocates breaking tasks into smaller, manageable segments, making initiating these fragments more achievable. The core principle here is not the pursuit of perfection but the initiation of action, transcending the inertia that procrastination often inflicts.

This concept isn't merely about swift action but also about creating a conducive environment for productivity. It advocates identifying and managing the triggers that lead to delay, whether from fear, overwhelm, or the quest for perfection. By acknowledging and addressing these triggers, individuals are better equipped to navigate the psychological barriers often accompanying procrastination.

Moreover, "Achieve It Now" encourages cultivating positive habits that counteract the allure of procrastination. It emphasizes the creation of routines and rituals that prime individuals for productivity, nurturing a conducive atmosphere for immediate action. By developing these proactive habits, individuals pave a path toward consistent and sustained progress.

The "Achieve It Now" concept is an antidote to procrastination's complexities. Fostering a mindset of immediate action, breaking tasks into manageable portions, and cultivating proactive habits serve as transformative tools to combat the entanglements of delay and pave the way for a more prolific and fulfilling approach to task completion.

2 UNVEILING THE COSTS OF DELAY

*"The cost of procrastination is the life not lived." - Leo
Babauta.*

Leo Babauta's poignant words resound deeply within the corridors of my journey, echoing in the uncharted territories affected by the procrastination web. I vividly recall a pivotal moment where a seemingly minor decision to postpone a critical project unraveled into a web of consequences far beyond the immediate delay. What initially appeared as a harmless deferral of a deadline metamorphosed into a chain reaction, disrupting the harmony of my personal and professional life. The delayed project impacted my work and seeped into moments with loved ones, causing undue stress and an undercurrent of unfulfilled commitments. This experience catalyzed a more profound exploration into the multifaceted costs incurred through procrastination. It's not merely about missed deadlines but the unquantifiable toll it takes on the fabric of life. Let us delve deeper into the layers of these hidden costs, exploring the intricate aftermath of delay in both personal and professional spheres.

2.1 TANGIBLE AND INTANGIBLE COSTS

The costs of procrastination manifest in a dual nature—both tangible and intangible—leaving an indelible mark on personal and professional realms. Let us explore this in detail.

- **Tangible Costs:** These are the concrete, measurable repercussions of procrastination. For instance, missed deadlines in the professional sphere often result in financial penalties, loss of potential income, or damage to one's professional reputation. Let's say a project deadline was delayed due to procrastination, resulting in financial penalties or even the loss of a lucrative contract. In personal finance, delaying bill payments can lead to late fees, impacting one's budget. Tangible costs manifest as missed opportunities or reduced productivity, leading to decreased income or growth.

- **Intangible Costs:** These are the less quantifiable yet deeply impactful consequences of procrastination. In my personal life, procrastination might strain relationships. Imagine delaying a vital conversation or failing to follow through on commitments, leading to eroded trust or disappointment in personal relationships. Emotionally, it can lead to increased stress, anxiety, and a sense of unfulfillment. Procrastination can generate a cycle of negative emotions, diminishing one's confidence and satisfaction. It can damage credibility and reliability professionally, impacting future opportunities or promotions.

For instance, let's consider a scenario where procrastination in meeting commitments gradually erodes trust and credibility in a work environment. This can impede career growth, diminish opportunities for advancement, or hinder collaborative prospects. Moreover, the stress generated by procrastination can negatively impact mental and emotional well-being, potentially affecting overall productivity and quality of life.

By understanding both the tangible and intangible costs, individuals can better grasp the holistic impact of procrastination beyond missed deadlines or delayed tasks, acknowledging the emotional, relational, and professional toll it takes.

Let us explore detailed real-life examples. These real-life stories exemplify how delayed actions due to procrastination can have tangible and intangible consequences, affecting professional opportunities, personal fulfillment, and overall life satisfaction.

- **Professional Consequences:** A marketing executive consistently delayed submitting proposals for new marketing campaigns. These delays seemed inconsequential initially but accumulated into missed opportunities over time. As marketing executive procrastinated, other marketing firms promptly presented their proposals. This led to losing potential clients, damaging the company's reputation and revenue. The delay in action directly impacted the firm's growth, and his professional reputation suffered. His delay didn't just affect one instance; it created a pattern that diminished his reliability and credibility, hindering her career progression and professional relationships.

- **Personal Consequences:** Consider the story of my friend, a passionate writer who had dreamed of penning a novel for years. However, my friend continuously postponed this endeavor for various reasons—lack of time, fear of failure, or waiting for the perfect moment. Years slipped away, and the novel remained unwritten. When my friend finally started writing, it was evident that the delay resulted in missed opportunities. The procrastination cost my friend's time, potential success, and personal fulfillment. There was a realization that the delay robbed the chance to share their stories with the world sooner, impacting their work's potential reach and impact.

2.2 CONFRONTING PROCRASTINATION COSTS

The following strategies will confront and address the hidden costs of procrastination.

1. **Awareness through Real-life Examples:** By seeing the consequences in others' lives, you might recognize patterns and potential repercussions in their experiences.

2. **Visualization of Potential Outcomes:** Visualize your potential future and imagine the achievements, successes, and personal fulfillment you could attain if you tackle procrastination. Conversely, it would help if you also visualized the potential setbacks and unfulfilled aspirations resulting from continued procrastination.

3. **Highlighting the Cumulative Effect:** Understand how small, repeated delays accumulate into significant consequences over time. Thinking about what might seem insignificant in the short term can snowball into more significant setbacks and missed opportunities in the long run.

4. **Empowerment through Action:** Take small steps immediately. Identify one task you have postponed and commit to completing, emphasizing the satisfaction and relief that follow

the action. This instills a sense of control and empowerment.

5. **Accountability and Support:** Share your goals and progress with someone you trust. This social support system can give you accountability and encouragement, making it easier to confront procrastination and its costs.

6. **Setting Clear Goals and Deadlines:** Set achievable goals with realistic deadlines. Breaking tasks into smaller, manageable steps can reduce the likelihood of procrastination.

By employing these strategies, you can better comprehend the hidden costs of procrastination and, in turn, feel motivated to take proactive steps to address and mitigate these costs.

It is of the utmost importance to place a strong emphasis on the transformative potential of recognizing and addressing the costs that are incurred as a result of delay brought on by procrastination. It is the first step toward reclaiming control over one's actions and shaping a more intentional and fulfilling path if one can recognize these costs. The accounts above of a marketing executive and a friend of mine who is a writer, as well as the investigation of hidden costs, serve as compelling reminders of the real impact that procrastination can have on a person's personal and professional life.

This chapter's objective is not to incite fear but to motivate action by shedding light on the consequences of procrastination. People can change their course from procrastination by employing newly acquired knowledge to drive transformation. As this section of the book draws close, the stage is set for you to embark on a more proactive and intentional approach to your endeavors. This will allow you to ensure that the hidden delay costs are acknowledged, confronted, and minimized in your pursuit of personal and professional fulfillment.

3 THE ANATOMY OF PROCRASTINATION

"Procrastination is the art of keeping up with yesterday."
- Don Marquis.

Don Marquis' poignant quote resonates deeply in procrastination, unveiling its intricate nature. The tendrils of procrastination wrapped around a project I held dear, a written endeavor that echoed my passion. What started as a manageable delay soon unraveled into a maze of psychological intricacies. The initial postponement of a crucial phase swiftly metamorphosed into a cycle of hesitation, cloaked in the guise of '**I will do it later**.' This experience became a mirror into the complexities of procrastination's anatomy, offering a profound insight into its underlying mechanisms. It wasn't merely a delay in tasks but a revelation of the emotional nuances and ingrained habits that underpin this intricate dance. As I navigated this labyrinth, it became evident that procrastination is more than a simple postponement; it's a tangle of emotions, habit, and the subtle allure of comfortable delay, hindering immediate action and nurturing a cycle that keeps us entangled in the past.

3.1 PSYCHOLOGY OF PROCRASTINATION

The psychological aspects behind procrastination are multifaceted, delving into the intricate workings of the human mind and emotions. They encompass various elements that contribute to this habit.

1. **Fear of Failure or Perfectionism:** Procrastination often stems from the fear of not meeting one's high standards. This perfectionistic tendency can delay tasks until conditions feel 'perfect' for execution, resulting in inertia due to an intense fear of failure.

2. **Instant Gratification vs. Long-term Goals:** The human brain is wired to seek immediate rewards. Procrastination occurs when short-term satisfaction (like watching TV or using social media) takes precedence over long-term goals, causing a delay in activities that don't provide immediate gratification.

3. **Emotional Regulation:** Procrastination can be a coping mechanism for managing negative emotions like stress, anxiety, or boredom. By postponing tasks, individuals temporarily avoid the discomfort associated with the task.

4. **Task Aversion and Overwhelm:** Procrastination often arises when a task seems daunting or overwhelming. Individuals may delay tasks that seem complex, leading to a feeling of being unable to tackle them effectively.

5. **Self-Regulation and Impulse Control:** Procrastination is linked to self-regulation and impulse control difficulties. This includes challenges in prioritizing tasks, managing time effectively, and resisting immediate distractions.

6. **Lack of Clarity and Decision Paralysis:** When the path forward is unclear, or there are too many options available, individuals may postpone decisions or actions, waiting for a more precise direction or avoiding making decisions due to the fear of making the wrong choice.

Understanding these psychological aspects aids in recognizing the root causes of procrastination and allows individuals to address these underlying factors. By acknowledging these aspects, individuals can employ strategies to overcome procrastination, whether through breaking tasks into smaller, manageable steps, creating structured plans, addressing perfectionistic tendencies, or developing emotional coping mechanisms. Emotional triggers and thought patterns play significant roles in contributing to procrastination.

1. **Fear of Failure:** The fear of not meeting personal or external expectations can paralyze action. For instance, someone might delay starting a project due to the fear of not delivering perfect results, leading to procrastination.

2. **Lack of Confidence:** When individuals lack self-belief or confidence in their abilities, they might postpone tasks that challenge their competence. For example, someone is postponing a job application due to feeling unqualified.

3. **Overwhelming and Stress:** Overwhelming tasks or high-stress levels can trigger procrastination. For instance, a student may delay studying for an exam due to the perceived enormity of the material, leading to avoidance behaviors.

4. **Perceived Lack of Control:** When individuals feel they lack control over a situation or task, they might procrastinate to regain control. For instance, someone might delay making a career decision when uncertain about the future.

5. **Instant Gratification and Distractions:** The allure of immediate pleasure or distractions can lead to procrastination. For example, we spend excessive time on social media instead of completing a tedious work assignment.

6. **Perfectionism:** Striving for perfection can delay tasks until they can be executed flawlessly. This might manifest in someone continually delaying the launch of a creative project due to the quest for perfection.

Recognizing these emotional triggers and thought patterns is crucial in addressing procrastination. By understanding how these triggers influence behavior, individuals can develop strategies to mitigate their effects, such as breaking tasks into smaller, more manageable parts, setting realistic goals, addressing fears, or employing time-management techniques to reduce stress and overwhelm.

3.2 REFLECT FOR PROCRASTINATION INSIGHT

Encouraging self-reflection on personal procrastination tendencies is crucial for understanding and addressing this habit. Here are methods to foster self-reflection.

1. **Journaling:** Encourage individuals to maintain a procrastination journal. They can note when and why they procrastinate, associated emotions or thoughts, and eventual outcomes. Reflecting on these entries provides insights into their patterns and triggers.

2. **Identifying Patterns:** Encourage individuals to recognize recurring behaviors or situations that trigger procrastination. Understanding common patterns helps in pre-emptively addressing or managing these triggers.

3. **Setting Aside Time for Reflection:** Allocate dedicated time to reflect on past experiences of

procrastination. This could involve reviewing missed opportunities, the emotional toll of delay, or the impact of procrastination on various aspects of life.

4. **Self-questioning:** Encourage probing questions, such as "What emotions or thoughts lead me to procrastinate?" or "What situations consistently trigger my delay?" This prompts deep introspection into personal procrastination tendencies.

5. **Assessing Consequences:** Reflect on the impact of procrastination. Ask individuals to consider how it affects their goals, well-being, and relationships. Understanding the actual costs motivates change.

6. **Seeking Feedback:** Encourage individuals to seek feedback from trusted sources. Others' observations might offer new perspectives on procrastination tendencies.

Through these self-reflection methods, individuals gain a deeper understanding of their procrastination tendencies, delay triggers, and impact on their lives. This insight empowers them to develop strategies to combat procrastination and foster more proactive behaviors.

Exploring the anatomy of procrastination presents an opportunity for you to embark on a transformative self-discovery journey. By unraveling the emotional triggers, thought patterns, and the labyrinthine complexities contributing to this habit, individuals gain a profound understanding of their procrastination tendencies.

This chapter is the foundation for self-reflection, prompting you to look deeply into your behaviors and their reasons. It is not simply an analysis of procrastination but rather a call to introspection and an attempt to comprehend the underlying psychological currents shaping their actions. With this comprehension comes the power to initiate change, paving the way for individuals to reclaim control over their actions and navigate away from the grip of procrastination. You can forge a path toward a more intentional, proactive, and fulfilling tomorrow due to the insight gained through this exploration, which provides the groundwork for developing personalized strategies and approaches.

4   THE DECISION TO CHANGE

"The secret of getting ahead is getting started." - Mark Twain.

When contemplating the crossroads of change and decision-making, the insightful words of Mark Twain ring loud and clear in the ear. There was a time when I was at the height of change, facing the chasm separating procrastination and forward movement. In one of these situations, the alluring delusion of **'later'** cast a shadow over a project that held tremendous personal significance for me. It was a moment that demanded a choice: to give in to the convenience of postponing the decision or to welcome the change. As I struggled under the burden of indecision, the profound insight gradually dawned on me that change did not solely rest in the hands of destiny but rather in the momentous decision that was made. This personal experience served as a testament to the profound impact of decisions in overcoming procrastination, highlighting the transformative power of the choice to get started. Here are practical strategies for breaking free from procrastination.

1. **Structured Planning:** Make specific timetables and to-do lists, as appropriate. Increasing the difficulty of a task while simultaneously decreasing its overwhelming nature can be accomplished by

breaking it down into a series of smaller, more manageable steps.

2. **Setting Clear Goals:** Define attainable and time-bound goals. The clarity that comes from having well-defined goals makes it much simpler to get started on various projects.

3. **Utilizing Time-Management Techniques:** Consider implementing time management strategies such as the Pomodoro Method, time blocking, or the Two-Minute Rule. These strategies are helpful in effectively managing one's time and overcoming the inertia of starting new tasks.

4. **Overcoming Perfectionism:** Accept that tasks don't need to be flawless. Embracing imperfection can release the pressure to procrastinate for fear of not meeting perfectionistic standards.

5. **Accountability Partners or Groups:** Motivating and encouraging others through accountability partners or support systems is possible. It is easier to stay committed and driven when one shares their goals and progress with others.

6. **Embracing the "Just Start" Mindset:** Beginning work, even for a few minutes. Getting started is frequently the most challenging part of any endeavor. Once something is started, it is

much easier to keep going as the momentum builds.

7. **Rewarding Progress:** Implement a system of rewards for completing tasks or reaching milestones. Positive reinforcement can motivate continued action.

8. **Mindfulness and Self-compassion:** Mindfulness meditation or self-compassion exercises can reduce anxiety and perfectionism, fostering a more forgiving and forward-thinking mindset.

By incorporating these practical strategies, individuals can actively confront procrastination tendencies and gradually develop a more proactive approach to their tasks and goals.

4.1 POWER OF DECISION-MAKING

The power of decision-making and commitment to change plays a pivotal role in combatting procrastination. Here's an in-depth explanation with examples.

1. **Initiating Change through Decisive Action:** Deciding to change involves taking the first step, often the most challenging one. For instance, deciding to start a fitness routine or commit to regular writing involves a conscious choice to act, breaking the cycle of procrastination.

2. **Consistency in Effort:** Commitment is essential in sustaining change. For instance, individuals committed to improving their writing skills allocate a set time each day to write, sticking to this routine despite initial challenges or distractions.

3. **Overcoming Inertia:** Decision-making coupled with commitment counteracts inertia. For instance, deciding to start a project or a task even when feeling unmotivated leads to a gradual build-up of momentum, making subsequent actions easier.

4. **Building New Habits:** Individuals can form new, productive habits through consistent decision-making and commitment. For example, deciding to start a daily meditation practice and sticking to it gradually transforms it into a regular habit.

5. **Resilience in the Face of Setbacks:** Commitment to change involves overcoming obstacles. For instance, after missing a writing day, the commitment to the goal keeps the individual from abandoning the entire writing routine.

6. **Transforming Mindset and Attitude:** The power of decision-making and commitment reshapes mindset and attitude towards tasks. It

fosters a proactive approach, shifting from **"I will do it later"** to **"I will start now."**

7. **Seeing Results and Progress:** Commitment and consistent decision-making lead to visible progress, reinforcing the efficacy of the chosen path. Witnessing improvements encourages sustained commitment.

The power of decision-making and unwavering commitment to change underscores the transformative potential within individuals. Individuals initiate and sustain change through these acts, cultivating new habits, overcoming inertia, and fostering a more proactive and purposeful approach to their goals and tasks.

4.2 PRACTICAL EXERCISE TO OVERCOME PROCRASTINATION

Individuals interested in making the first steps toward transformation may find the following exercises helpful, particularly in overcoming procrastination.

1. **Creating a Procrastination Log:** Keep a log in which you record each instance of procrastination that you engage in. Include specifics like the triggers, feelings, and length of delay in your explanation. This log reveals personal patterns and triggers, which can help make decisions.

2. **Goal Setting and Time Blocking:** Establish measurable, attainable objectives, and then schedule blocks of time to focus exclusively on achieving those objectives. Doing so creates a structured approach, strengthening one's commitment to beginning and completing tasks.

3. **Implementing the Two-Minute Rule:** Getting started immediately with a task that can be completed in fewer than two minutes. For example, I cleaned up a small area or responded to a brief email. This helps to build momentum while also lowering the barrier to entry.

4. **Visualization Exercises:** Visualize the positive outcomes of completing a task and the negative consequences of procrastinating. This exercise motivates action by creating a vivid mental image of success.

5. **Setting a Clear Action Plan:** Break down larger tasks into smaller, manageable steps. Outline a clear action plan with specific milestones. This exercise fosters a practical path forward.

6. **Implementation Intentions:** Implement intentions by planning the 'when' and 'where' of task execution. For example, "When I finish breakfast, I will start working on the report in my home office."

7. **Mindfulness Practices:** Mindfulness practices can help one become more aware of what is happening here and now. Recognizing the factors that contribute to procrastination and refocusing attention on the task at hand are both facilitated by this practice.

These exercises aim to initiate a proactive shift in behavior by instigating small, manageable steps. By implementing these exercises, individuals gain practical strategies to overcome the inertia of procrastination and set themselves on a path toward transformation and sustained change.

The power to change is in your hands and choices. One must commit to changing behavior and take the necessary steps. This chapter should inspire you to use your decisions and commitments to fight procrastination. These exercises and strategies give you a transformation roadmap by making small but deliberate changes. A proactive, purposeful, and transformative journey can begin with each decision and commitment. No matter how small, the first steps start a powerful and lasting transformation to overcome procrastination.

5 BUILDING PROACTIVE HABITS

"The secret of your future is hidden in your daily routine." - Mike Murdock.

This illuminating remark by Mike Murdock captures the essence of proactive habits and their profound impact on our lives. As I reflected on my journey to overcome procrastination, a defining moment highlighted the transformative power of developing new habits. A new realm of possibilities was revealed to me when I consciously introduced proactive behaviors and gradually altered my routine to accommodate these changes. One such instance was when I made a concerted effort to devote the first hour of each day to working without interruption and with complete concentration. This seemingly insignificant change was critical in reshaping not only my level of productivity but also my overall approach to the tasks at hand. This individual investigation into the formation of habits highlighted the transformative potential that can be found within daily routines. It also highlighted the pivotal role that proactive habits play in steering us away from the allure of procrastination and toward a more purposeful, efficient, and fulfilling life.

5.1 PROACTIVE HABITS

It serves as a potent antidote to the lingering grip of procrastination. Here's a detailed explanation along with a practical example.

1. **Structured Daily Routines:** Establishing a structured daily routine is a cornerstone of proactive habits. For example, dedicating the first hour of the morning to a specific, focused task becomes a customary practice. This structured routine sets the tone for a productive day, reducing the likelihood of succumbing to procrastination's allure.

2. **Time Blocking and Prioritization:** Implementing time blocking and prioritization exercises form proactive habits. By assigning specific time slots to tasks based on their importance, individuals become adept at managing their time effectively, reducing the tendency to postpone critical tasks.

3. **Consistent Goal Setting:** Embracing consistent goal setting becomes a proactive habit. This involves defining clear, achievable, and time-bound goals, thereby steering individuals toward regular progress and maintaining momentum, curtailing the space for procrastination.

4. **Implementation of the "Two-Minute Rule":** Employing the "Two-Minute Rule" as a customary

practice assists in initiating tasks that take less than two minutes immediately. This practice eliminates the inertia often associated with getting started, contributing to an ongoing proactive mindset.

5. **Mindful Work Breaks:** Incorporating mindful work breaks is customary. Short, scheduled breaks between tasks promote focus and refreshment, mitigating burnout and sustaining consistent work progress.

6. **Habitual Review and Reflection:** Regularly reviewing and reflecting on daily progress becomes a proactive habit. Evaluating completed tasks and setting goals for the following day cultivates a pattern of continuous improvement, reducing the tendency for procrastination to seep in.

Through habitual adoption of these proactive strategies, individuals create a framework that minimizes the space for procrastination to thrive. These habits gradually shape a proactive and purpose-driven approach to daily activities, bolstering focus, productivity, and forward momentum.

5.2 ROUTINE TO FOSTER PRODUCTIVITY

Here are guidelines and examples for creating a daily routine that fosters productivity.

1. **Define Clear Blocks of Time:** Allocate specific time blocks for different tasks. For instance, dedicate the first hour in the morning to focused work on the most critical task or project.

2. **Prioritize Tasks:** Create a priority list, focusing on high-value tasks. Prioritization ensures that essential tasks receive attention early in the day, decreasing the risk of procrastination.

3. **Use Technology Mindfully:** Schedule periods for checking emails and social media. For example, designate 15 minutes after lunch for responding to emails and limit social media browsing to specific breaks.

4. **Incorporate Mindfulness or Breaks:** Integrate short breaks or moments of mindfulness into the routine. Examples include a five-minute mindfulness exercise mid-morning and a brief walk in the afternoon to refresh and maintain focus.

5. **Create Consistent Work Environments:** Designate a dedicated workspace for tasks. A consistent environment signals the brain that it's time for focused work, enhancing productivity.

6. **Plan Time for Learning or Growth:** Allocate a segment for personal development, such as reading, learning new skills, or professional

growth. Schedule 30 minutes each evening for self-improvement activities.

7. **End-of-Day Reflection:** Close the day by reflecting on accomplishments and setting priorities for the next day. This reflection aids in celebrating achievements and preparing for the following day's tasks.

For instance, a daily routine could start with a focused hour of deep work on a significant project, followed by a short break for a mindful walk. Mid-morning could involve responding to emails, followed by a priority task, and then a break for learning or growth activities. Afternoon tasks may continue in the dedicated workspace, ending the day with a reflection and prioritization for the next day.

This structured routine not only fosters productivity but also acts as a shield against the intrusion of procrastination, allowing individuals to focus on their most critical tasks with increased efficiency. Here are tips and techniques for setting and achieving short-term goals.

1. **Specific and Measurable Goals:** Define goals with specific and measurable outcomes. For instance, instead of "exercise more," set a goal like "run for 20 minutes three times a week."

2. **Break Goals into Smaller Tasks:** Divide larger goals into smaller, manageable tasks. For example,

if the aim is to write a 5,000-word essay in a week, break it down into daily word count goals.

3. **Time-Bound Targets:** Set deadlines or time frames for each goal. For instance, I am committing to finish reading a book by the end of the month or submitting a report by Friday.

4. **Regular Progress Tracking:** Monitor progress regularly. Use tools like checklists or apps to track daily progress toward the goal.

5. **Flexibility and Adjustment:** Be open to adjusting goals as needed. Revise the schedule without compromising the overall objective if a task takes longer than expected.

6. **Positive Reinforcement:** Celebrate small milestones or accomplishments. This can be as simple as rewarding yourself after completing a task or hitting a specific milestone.

7. **Accountability and Support:** Share goals with someone who can support or hold you accountable. This can be a friend, colleague, or mentor.

For instance, a short-term goal might be to learn a new language. Breaking it into smaller tasks could involve completing daily specific lessons or vocabulary exercises. Setting a time-bound target could mean having basic conversations in that language within three months. Using a tracking app to monitor daily progress and celebrate reaching milestones, like completing a level in the language learning app, could provide positive reinforcement. Sharing progress with a language-learning buddy could offer accountability and support. These strategies and techniques contribute to a more structured and achievable approach to short-term goal setting, fostering consistent progress and reducing the likelihood of procrastination.

It's crucial to emphasize proactive habits and achievable goals' transformative power. In addition to increasing productivity, these strategies also protect against procrastination. This chapter leads to a more purposeful and focused daily routine with structured habits and goals. The chapter establishes a more purposeful and focused approach. These habits' transformative power lies in channeling an individual's energy and effort towards short-term goals, bringing them closer to their larger goals. These practices show the importance of a proactive mindset to avoid procrastination and create a future of intentional action and accomplishment.

6 OVERCOMING PROCRASTINATION TRIGGERS

"The secret of change is to focus all of your energy, not on fighting the old, but on building the new." – Socrates.

Socrates' timeless wisdom rings true in the complex tapestry of battling procrastination triggers. My journey navigating the labyrinth of procrastination revealed a pivotal moment when I recognized the significance of addressing triggers. It was a project deadline fast approaching, yet the pull of procrastination whispered tantalizing excuses, inviting delay. As I reflect, one standout experience emerges - the intersection of overwhelming tasks and the fear of failure. This intersection became a breeding ground for procrastination. The compulsion to put off daunting tasks in favor of comfort became a familiar refrain. Understanding this trigger and actively redirecting energy toward a solution unveiled the power to break free from the shackles of procrastination. This introspective journey emphasized the profound significance of understanding and overcoming triggers to lay the groundwork for a future not bound by procrastination's grip.

6.1 TRIGGERS OF PROCRASTINATION

Identifying common triggers of procrastination is crucial in combating this habit. Here are some common triggers and methods to recognize them.

1. **Overwhelm:** When tasks appear too numerous, complex, or substantial, a person may experience a feeling of being unable to manage or initiate the tasks. This is known as "overwhelm." However, by becoming aware of feelings of immobility, stress, or the compulsion to flee from an activity. This sensation can be brought on by many tasks or the sheer magnitude of a project.

2. **Fear:** Procrastination can be caused by fear of failing or succeeding and the unknown. However, recognizing feelings of apprehension, resistance, or perfectionistic tendencies leads to inaction because of their paralyzing effect. The inability to start or complete a task could be one of the manifestations of fear.

3. **Lack of Clarity:** Procrastination is a typical result of having tasks that are unclear or ambiguous in some way. People can put off tasks because they are unsure how to get started or what is expected. They are feeling lost or uncertain about how to begin a task or a lack of understanding about what is required to complete the task.

4. **Perfectionism:** Procrastination can result from striving for perfection because it causes one to put off completing tasks out of an overwhelming desire for them to be perfect. The constant repetition of work or an excessive focus on minute details, both of which cause a delay in the completion of tasks.

5. **Lack of Motivation:** A lack of interest or motivation in a task is one of the potential causes of procrastination. The inability to begin or persist with a task because of a lack of interest in the activity or a sensation of being bored with it.

6. **Distractions:** Procrastination can be significantly aided by distractions from the outside world, such as social media, notifications, or environmental factors. When confronted with a significant task or a deadline, I experience a strong urge to check social media, browse the internet, or concentrate on less critical tasks.

7. **Indecision:** Delays can occur when making decisions or choosing a strategy to implement to complete a difficult task. We spend excessive time thinking about potential courses of action without beginning the task or vacillating between different methods.

8. **Lack of Structure:** Procrastination is a typical result of approaching a task unorganized or

unstructured. Problems organizing tasks can lead to a lack of clarity regarding how to get started or where to go from there.

Recognizing these triggers involves introspection and self-awareness. By identifying these common triggers - overwhelm, fear, lack of clarity, and perfectionism - individuals gain insight into their procrastination patterns, allowing them to proactively address and overcome these barriers. Here are strategies and examples for managing and overcoming various triggers of procrastination.

1. **Overwhelm:** Separate each task into smaller, more manageable steps. If you are working on a complicated project, divide it into manageable parts or milestones and set specific due dates for each section.

2. **Fear:** Shift your perspective on what failure and success mean. Recognize that mistakes are a necessary part of the learning process and that achieving success requires drawing wisdom from past mistakes.

3. **Lack of Clarity**: Seek clarification and make sure your task lists and plans are crystal clear. If you are unsure how to complete a task, seeking direction from someone else or additional information is best.

4. **Perfectionism:** Establish goals that can be achieved and be willing to accept failure. Instead of producing flawless work, you should strive to finish and improve the project in small, incremental steps.

5. **Lack of Motivation:** To get the ball rolling, take baby steps that are easily accomplished. When tackling a challenging project, it's best to start with the least complicated part and build up your motivation as you go.

6. **Distractions:** Establish a setting free of distractions and schedule blocks of time during which you will be able to concentrate. Turn off notifications, set aside specific times for focused work, and get rid of any other distractions that may be present.

7. **Indecision:** Place time constraints on the decision-making process and embrace a "good enough" mentality. When considering your choices, it is helpful to set a time limit for making a decision and remember that making any decision is preferable to making none.

8. **Lack of Structure:** Make detailed schedules and to-do lists to give yourself some structure. When organizing and prioritizing tasks, tools such as calendars, to-do lists, or project management applications can be helpful.

Applying these strategies, individuals can effectively manage and overcome the various triggers of procrastination. These examples demonstrate actionable steps to counteract each trigger, fostering a proactive and focused approach toward tasks and goals.

6.2 CULTIVATE RESILIENCE

Here are ways to cultivate resilience in procrastination challenges and corresponding examples.

1. **Mindfulness and Self-Compassion:** Through practicing mindfulness, one can learn to identify the factors that lead to procrastination without engaging in self-criticism. When dealing with procrastination, it is essential to recognize the cause without being overly critical of oneself to cultivate a more self-compassionate attitude.

2. **Learning from Setbacks:** Consider the obstacles you face as opportunities for growth rather than failures. Reflect on why you put off completing a task in the first place, apply what you've learned from the experience, and modify your strategy for the next task based on what you've learned.

3. **Time Management and Prioritization:** Master the art of time management and effectively prioritize your responsibilities. Develop a systematic plan in which you set aside specific

amounts of time for essential activities and forestall the onset of procrastination.

4. **Embracing Imperfection:** The path to happiness is accepting progress over pursuing perfection. Realize that completing tasks does not need to be perfect; instead, the objective is to perform them adequately while continuously improving.

5. **Positive Mindset and Resilient Attitude:** Develop a constructive mentality and a tenacious approach to overcoming obstacles. Instead of meditating on procrastinations of the past, you should adopt a forward-focused, problem-solving approach for upcoming tasks.

6. **Continuous Self-Reflection:** Participate in regular periods of self-reflection to understand your patterns and behaviors. Evaluate your routines, what causes you to procrastinate, and how you react to them regularly so that you can adjust your strategies accordingly.

7. **Seeking Support and Accountability:** Find a support group or a person you can be accountable to to keep moving forward. Discussing your objectives with a guide, a close friend, or a coworker can provide support and help you stay accountable.

Developing resilience involves a blend of self-awareness, adaptive strategies, and a positive mindset. These examples showcase approaches to fortify one's resilience in the face of procrastination challenges, enabling individuals to confront setbacks and persist in their efforts to overcome procrastination habits.

Resilience is critical to overcoming procrastination triggers. Resilience and adaptability can help people overcome procrastination. This chapter showed the power of mindfulness, self-compassion, and learning from mistakes, laying the groundwork for navigating procrastination triggers with empathy and self-awareness.

The journey toward resilience involves a shift in perspective, embracing imperfections, and viewing challenges as opportunities for growth. It's not solely about evading procrastination but learning from it, leveraging each setback as a stepping stone toward personal and professional development.

With time management, prioritization, and positivity strategies, people can move from self-criticism to self-reflection and growth. This chapter concludes by promoting a culture of continuous learning and adapting and promoting resilience as the key to overcoming procrastination and personal growth.

7 THE JOURNEY TO RESILIENCE

"The gem cannot be polished without friction, nor man perfected without trials." - Chinese Proverb.

The words of this ancient proverb resonate deeply in the realm of combating procrastination and fostering resilience. Reflecting on my journey, I encountered a moment that encapsulated the essence of resilience in the face of procrastination's challenges. It was a time when the weight of procrastination seemed impossible, and the looming deadlines cast a formidable shadow. In the depths of this struggle, a realization emerged - the necessity of resilience as a tool to navigate the labyrinth of procrastination. This chapter is a testament to the transformative power of resilience, a quality not formed in comfort but honed in the face of adversity. Embracing these trials as opportunities for growth, this journey unfolds as a guide to fortify resilience, enabling the triumph over the grip of procrastination.

7.1 RESILIENCE FOR PROCRASTINATION

Resilience plays a pivotal role in conquering the challenges of procrastination. Here is a comprehensive understanding of resilience and its significance in overcoming procrastination.

Resilience is the ability to adapt and bounce back from setbacks, challenges, and adversity. It involves navigating difficulties, stress, or failures without being overwhelmed or deviating from one's path. When applied to procrastination, resilience becomes the tool that enables individuals to face the setbacks caused by procrastination without losing focus or motivation.

1. **Mindfulness and Self-Awareness:** Resilience starts with self-awareness. Mindfulness of procrastination patterns and triggers is the initial step toward building resilience.

2. **Learning from Setbacks:** Resilient individuals view procrastination setbacks as learning experiences. They analyze the reasons behind procrastination and use these insights to adjust their approach for future tasks.

3. **Positive Mindset and Problem-Solving Attitude:** Resilience in procrastination involves maintaining a positive outlook and a problem-solving attitude. Instead of fixating on the delay, resilient individuals focus on solutions and the way forward.

4. **Adaptability and Flexibility:** Adapting to change plans or approaches when faced with procrastination challenges is a sign of resilience. Individuals who adapt their strategies to suit different situations display stronger resilience in combating procrastination.

5. **Seeking Support and Building a Support System:** Building a support network helps maintain resilience in the face of procrastination. Seeking guidance or support from mentors, friends, or colleagues aids in staying accountable and motivated.

Developing resilience involves building coping mechanisms, fostering a positive mindset, and leveraging setbacks as opportunities for growth. It's about maintaining composure and adaptability when faced with procrastination triggers, fostering a solid foundation to confront and overcome these challenges. Let me share with you the stories of world-famous personalities.

- **Mahatma Gandhi:** Known as the "Father of the Nation," Mohandas Karamchand Gandhi's initial years were marked by struggles with self-discipline. His schooling and legal studies in London were fraught with procrastination and self-doubt. However, after undergoing transformative experiences in South Africa and delving into philosophical texts, he developed a disciplined routine, adhering to ethical principles and committing himself to social causes. His resilience and commitment to nonviolent resistance led India to independence, leaving an indelible mark on the world.

- **A.P.J. Abdul Kalam:** Fondly remembered as the "Missile Man of India," Dr. Kalam overcame academic setbacks and financial difficulties in his youth. Through unwavering dedication and a profound love for science, he pursued a career in aerospace engineering. His journey from being a paperboy to becoming the 11th President of India showcased his unyielding spirit and commitment to learning. His simplicity and vision continue to inspire generations.

- **Ratan Tata:** As the scion of the Tata family, Ratan Tata inherited a vast industrial conglomerate. However, he encountered hurdles during the early years of his leadership. Tata faced challenges in steering the group through economic uncertainties and global competition. His visionary leadership and unconventional decisions drove the company's expansion and global prominence. His approach emphasized innovation, ethical business practices, and social responsibility, leaving an enduring legacy in the corporate world.

These individuals' stories exemplify how resilience, determination, and a commitment to personal development can lead to remarkable achievements, serving as beacons of inspiration for future generations.

7.2 ENHANCE RESILIENCE

Here are some practical exercises and methods to enhance resilience.

1. **Mindfulness and Meditation:** To maintain your presence at the moment and your composure in the face of challenging circumstances, engage in mindfulness practices such as deep breathing, meditation, or yoga. To help you find your center amidst the stress in your life, try devoting 10–15 minutes of each day to deep breathing or mindfulness meditation.

2. **Self-Reflection and Journaling:** Write about difficult experiences, reflect on how you responded to them, and note what you discovered. After you have made a mistake because you procrastinated, write in a journal about what happened, how you felt about it, and how you can avoid repeating the same mistake.

3. **Setting Realistic Goals:** To complete more significant tasks, larger tasks should be broken down into smaller, more manageable goals, which should be realistic and measurable. Instead of finishing an entire project in one sitting, try breaking it down into smaller, more manageable tasks with specific due dates.

4. **Seek Support and Build a Network:** Put yourself in a position to receive guidance and

inspiration by surrounding yourself with a supportive community of people, whether friends, mentors, or professionals. Participate in workshops, try to find a mentor, or sign up for peer support groups to strengthen your support network.

5. **Adaptability and Flexibility:** When confronted with challenges, try shaking up your routines or taking a different approach. Be flexible in your approach to completing a task, and consider using a different tactic if the one you had planned doesn't produce the desired results.

6. **Positive Self-Talk and Affirmations:** Use positive self-talk to encourage and motivate yourself in challenging situations. Repeat affirmations such as "I learn and grow from setbacks" or "I am capable of overcoming obstacles" to reinforce resilience.

7. **Physical Well-being and Stress Management:** To maintain resiliency and manage stress, it is essential to exercise regularly, make sleep a priority, and eat a balanced diet. As stress management, make it a habit to participate in some form of physical activity daily or schedule regular breaks at work during which you can stretch and unwind.

These practical exercises are designed to bolster resilience in the face of procrastination challenges, fostering a mindset and approach that enables individuals to confront setbacks and emerge stronger.

We conclude this resilience exploration by acknowledging its crucial role in fighting procrastination. Resilience guides procrastinators through the maze. The stories of great people, practical exercises, and lessons learned emphasize resilience. Setbacks become stepping stones with resilience, adaptability, and perseverance. Resilience can transform procrastination, as shown in this chapter. Self-discovery, support, and adaptability form a solid foundation to overcome procrastination and grow personally.

8 A PROCRASTINATION-FREE FUTURE

"The future belongs to those who prepare for it today." -
Malcolm X.

These words encapsulate the spirit of the journey I have been on to conquer my tendency to put things off until later. There was a time when the grasp of delay encumbered my aspirations, weaving a web of uncertainty around the path that led to my goals and aspirations. Those days are long gone. The defining moment that pushed me to make changes in my life was when I realized that the future I had envisioned for myself was being lost in the mists of time under the guise of "tomorrow." This realization was the impetus for me to make changes. My awareness of the need to confront this pattern of behavior directly was heightened when I was placed in an environment where the allure of procrastination cast a shadow over each day. This chapter acts as a guidepost by illuminating a future free of procrastination and serving as a reference point. It weaves the threads of personal experiences, strategies honed through trials, and the vision of a future unbound by the constraints that procrastination imposes on the future.

8.1 BENEFITS OF PROCRASTINATION-FREE LIFE

To "paint a vivid picture of a life free from procrastination," one must illustrate the transformation and benefits of leading a life free from procrastination.

1. **Enhanced Productivity and Achievement:** Living without procrastination enables individuals to accomplish more quickly. Talk about the effectiveness, the increased productivity, and the satisfaction that results from finishing tasks promptly.

2. **Reduced Stress and Anxiety:** Bring attention to the fact that doing away with procrastination helps reduce stress and anxiety, which in turn contributes to a state of mind that is more balanced and peaceful. Talk about the release and mental clarity of not putting off tasks.

3. **Improved Relationships and Well-being:** Describe the positive effects of overcoming procrastination on one's relationships and overall well-being. Describe how reducing stress and feeling accomplished can improve interpersonal relationships and a more fulfilling life.

4. **Personal Growth and Confidence:** Demonstrate how overcoming procrastination contributes to personal development and increases self-confidence. Explain how developing the

routine of completing tasks promptly can lead to a greater sense of self-worth and accomplishment.

5. **Clear Vision and Goal Attainment:** Place emphasis on having a crystal clear vision and the ability to set and accomplish goals without allowing procrastination to get in the way. Discuss the sense of empowerment and focus that comes from working toward and achieving one's goals as quickly as possible.

6. **Time for Self-Improvement and Enjoyment:** Call attention to the additional free time that can be created by eliminating procrastination. Discuss ways this additional time can be used to better oneself, pursue one's interests, or relax and enjoy oneself.

Illustrating this transformed life free from procrastination paints a picture of increased productivity, enhanced well-being, improved relationships, and the overall fulfillment that stems from seizing the present moment without delay. A procrastination-free existence significantly influences personal and professional growth, providing numerous benefits.

1. **Enhanced Time Management and Efficiency:** The effective management of time is hampered by procrastination. Eliminating procrastination from one's life leads to improved time management and increased effectiveness in

one's day-to-day activities, professional obligations, and personal pursuits.

2. **Increased Productivity and Performance:** Without the weight of procrastination on their shoulders, people can perform at their absolute best. The ability to meet deadlines becomes more manageable, productivity rises, and the quality of work improves, all of which contribute to increased professional success.

3. **Improved Decision-making and Confidence:** Individuals gain the ability to make prompt decisions and take assertive action when they can overcome their tendency to procrastinate. This increases confidence and self-assurance, which are essential in personal and professional development.

4. **Strengthened Relationships and Communication:** The prompt completion of tasks and reduced stress caused by procrastination make room for improved communication and the fortification of relationships. Because of this, productive collaborations and meaningful social connections are created.

5. **Continuous Learning and Adaptability:** Living a life free of procrastination helps to cultivate an environment that values lifelong education and flexibility. People consistently work

on bettering themselves, expanding their skill sets, and becoming more flexible in the face of shifting demands in their professional environments.

6. **Career Advancement and Personal Fulfillment:** Career advancement occurs when tasks are completed promptly, leading to accomplishment and personal fulfillment. This helps cultivate a positive work environment and a drive to achieve even greater things.

A life free from procrastination catalyzes professional growth by boosting productivity and performance and enhances personal development by fostering better time management, decision-making, and relationships. These combined benefits pave the way for an enriched and more fulfilling life.

8.2 PLAN, EXECUTE, EXCEL

Here is a more detailed elaboration on challenging you to envision and work towards a brighter future.

1. **Creating a Vision Board:** Encourage you to craft a vision board illustrating your goals and aspirations. This visual representation is a constant reminder of what they're working towards. For instance, if a reader aspires to start a business, their vision board might include images of successful entrepreneurs, business ideas, and growth charts.

2. **Developing a Personal Development Plan:** Prompt you to outline a personal development plan that encompasses short-term and long-term goals. For instance, if someone aims to advance in their career, the plan might include skill development, networking objectives, and career milestones.

3. **Practicing Visualization Techniques:** Encourage you to use visualization exercises. For instance, if someone desires a healthier lifestyle, they can visualize themselves exercising, eating healthily, and feeling energetic. This visualization technique helps create a mental image of the desired future.

4. **Setting Clear Objectives with Timelines:** Advocate for setting clear, measurable objectives with specific timelines. For instance, if a reader aims to write a book, setting a daily word count goal and a deadline for completion helps turn the vision into a tangible, actionable plan.

5. **Cultivating a Supportive Environment:** Suggest the importance of surrounding oneself with a supportive network. If a reader wants to delve into a new industry, connecting with mentors or joining relevant groups can provide guidance and support.

6. **Continuous Learning and Adaptation:** Encourage you to learn and adapt constantly. If someone envisions a career change, continuous learning and staying abreast of industry trends are vital steps to shape that future.

Empowering you to take these steps solidifies your vision and provides a structured approach to turning dreams into reality. The aim is to challenge you to take active steps, fostering a mindset and a practical strategy to achieve your envisioned future.

As we conclude this investigation into a procrastination-free future, we must acknowledge that our goals are achievable. Present decisions often determine success and potential. We can unlock our potential and aspirations by overcoming our procrastination. Let's advance our understanding, strategies, and visions from these pages. Let us take action and work toward the better tomorrow we envision at this crossroads between the past and the future. We must accept challenges, commit to the journey, and take proactive action to create our dream future. We must paint our lives masterpieces one proactive and decisive brushstroke at a time. Our future canvas awaits our strokes; let's paint our masterpieces.

9 CONCLUSION

"The journey of a thousand miles begins with a single step." - Lao Tzu.

As we culminate this transformative expedition through the intricate labyrinth of procrastination, it's crucial to reflect on the collective wisdom garnered from each chapter. This journey has been a testament to the resilient spirit that propels us towards progress and the choice to confront the covert habits that hinder our aspirations. Each chapter has unfurled a tapestry of insights, strategies, and personal anecdotes to equip us for a procrastination-free existence. The voyage embarked upon has not merely been about deciphering the enigmatic grip of procrastination; it's been a testament to the tenacity required to forge a brighter tomorrow. As we stand at this juncture, poised after this comprehensive guide, let us distill the wisdom gained into actionable steps, drawing from the lessons learned to propel us toward a future of unwavering determination and realized ambitions. The call to action beckons, urging us to take that step toward realizing our most ambitious dreams.

9.1 KEY TAKEAWAYS

Throughout the journey detailed in "Achieve It Now: Beat Procrastination for a Brighter Tomorrow," several key takeaways and pivotal lessons emerge.

1. **Understanding Procrastination's Grip:** Procrastination isn't just about delaying tasks; it's a complex habit rooted in various emotional triggers and misconceptions. Recognizing its nuances is essential for combating it effectively.

2. **Strategies for Overcoming Procrastination:** A wide variety of approaches, including the formation of proactive habits, the control of triggers, the promotion of resilience, the establishment of clear objectives, and the maintenance of consistent self-reflection.

3. **Power of Vision and Action:** Envisioning a procrastination-free future and taking consistent, actionable steps are foundational to breaking free from the grip of delay. This combination shapes the path to success and personal growth.

4. **Embracing Resilience and Adaptability:** The journey underscores the importance of resilience in the face of setbacks. Adapting to challenges and continuously learning are vital elements in navigating a life without procrastination.

5. **Importance of Decision-making and Commitment:** The power of decisive action and unwavering commitment to change plays a significant role in overcoming procrastination. Choosing to act is pivotal in shaping a more fulfilled life.

6. **Continuous Reflection and Growth:** For continuous introspection, gaining wisdom from one's experiences, and fostering an atmosphere that encourages personal and professional development.

7. **Proactive Mindset for a Brighter Future:** The call to action in envisioning a brighter tomorrow resonates with the need for a proactive mindset. Taking deliberate steps and consistent actions shape the destiny we aspire for.

8. **Value of Structured Routines and Goal-setting:** Structured daily routines and setting achievable short-term goals are instrumental in combating procrastination. These routines foster productivity and direction toward achieving larger aspirations.

9. **Benefits of Visualization and Planning:** Techniques such as visualization and detailed planning aid in materializing aspirations. Visualizing success and creating a comprehensive plan enhance the chances of achieving desired goals.

10. **Supportive Environment and Continuous Learning:** Surrounding oneself with a supportive network and fostering a culture of continuous learning and adaptability is pivotal in sustaining progress and navigating through challenges.

11. **Resilience in the Face of Setbacks:** The importance of resilience stands out as a crucial tool in overcoming setbacks and obstacles. Learning from failures and using them as stepping stones to success is a significant part of the journey.

12. **Balancing Personal and Professional Growth:** Promotes a healthy balance between personal and professional development. Both are necessary components of a life devoid of procrastination and lived to its full potential.

These takeaways collectively highlight the necessity of understanding procrastination's intricacies, the strategies for overcoming it, and the power of proactive action in shaping a fulfilling, procrastination-free future.

9.2 EMBRACE PROACTIVE MINDSET

Embracing a proactive mindset and defeating procrastination is pivotal for personal growth and success. It involves a deliberate and consistent commitment to action, fostering a mindset that empowers individuals to take charge of their lives.

1. **Seizing Opportunities and Making Decisions:** A proactive mindset encourages seizing opportunities as they arise, making decisions, and taking action rather than passively waiting. This approach ensures individuals control

their destinies, shaping their paths rather than being dictated by external circumstances.

2. **Cultivating a Culture of Action and Productivity:** Defeating procrastination requires fostering a culture of action and productivity. Proactive individuals understand the value of time and actively engage in tasks rather than postponing them. This culture of productivity propels them towards their goals.

3. **Commitment to Continuous Improvement:** A proactive mindset values continuous self-improvement. It involves consistent learning, adapting to changing environments, and embracing new challenges—this commitment to growth fuels progress and resilience in the face of setbacks.

4. **Harnessing the Power of Intent and Focus**: Proactive individuals harness the power of intent and focus, directing their energy towards specific goals. They prioritize their objectives and take calculated steps to achieve them, avoiding the traps of distraction and delay.

5. **Building Resilience and Overcoming Challenges:** A proactive mindset bolsters resilience, enabling individuals to bounce back from setbacks. It instills the belief that challenges are opportunities for growth rather than

insurmountable obstacles, encouraging a persistent pursuit of success.

6. **Crafting a Vision and Taking Action:** Proactive individuals don't merely envision their future; they actively pursue it. This involves mapping out a clear vision and consistently taking deliberate steps to transform that vision into reality.

Embracing a proactive mindset is integral to defeating procrastination. It empowers individuals to be the architects of their destinies, guiding them toward success, fulfillment, and a life free from the constraints of delay. It's not just about envisioning a brighter future; it's about actively working toward it.

Procrastination-free living requires courage, determination, and unwavering commitment to the complexities of life. Every step, every decision you make to overcome delay, and every ounce of resilience you show in the face of challenges move you closer to your dream life. Success is a journey, not an event; it's daily, deliberate steps. Take advantage of every opportunity to overcome procrastination and achieve your goals. Your efforts today create a future full of success and potential. Strive, persevere, and embrace your proactive side. Every step toward success is worthwhile. The destination is ahead, but the journey is fun—keep going!

I encourage you to embrace the journey, appreciate the progress made, and continue your pursuit of a procrastination-free, prosperous future is essential. It's about acknowledging that the efforts you put in each day, no matter how small, collectively pave the way for a fulfilling and successful life.

This transformative expedition ends with reflection and rebirth. In 'Achieve It Now', we learn how to overcome procrastination, shape destinies, and create a bright future. Remember the lessons from these chapters as we say goodbye. Daily, we use our wisdom, strategies, and dreams. Take advantage of every moment to stop procrastinating and live purposefully. That journey continues so we can paint our dreams in vibrant colors. Make the last page the start of life without delay, full of potential, and driven by the desire to create a future of lasting success and unwavering fulfillment.

I aim to inspire you to carry forward the wisdom and lessons from the book, urging you to continue your proactive journey toward a life liberated from procrastination with accomplishments and fulfillment.

10 APPENDIX

This Appendix delves deeper into supplementary materials and resources to further fortify your journey toward overcoming procrastination. Here, you will discover various tools, exercises, and additional insights to support your quest for a procrastination-free existence. These supplementary materials are designed to enhance your understanding, reinforce strategies, and equip you with additional resources to navigate the complexities of procrastination. From templates for goal setting to a curated list of further readings, this section serves as a treasure trove of aids to bolster your proactive approach towards a life teeming with achievements and personal growth. Embrace these resources as companions in your ongoing expedition to conquer procrastination and seize a brighter future. Here are some suggestions for additional resources and recommended readings for you.

Recommended Readings

1. "The Power of Habit: Why We Do What We Do in Life and Business" by Charles Duhigg

2. "Atomic Habits: An Easy & Proven Way to Build Good Habits & Break Bad Ones" by James Clear

3. "Deep Work: Rules for Focused Success in a Distracted World" by Cal Newport

4. "Mindset: The New Psychology of Success" by Carol S. Dweck

5. "The Now Habit: A Strategic Program for Overcoming Procrastination and Enjoying Guilt-Free Play" by Neil Fiore

Productivity Tools

1. Trello: For organizing tasks and setting up visual boards.
2. Forest App: To manage distractions and enhance focus through timed work sessions.
3. Habitica: Gamified task manager that turns your tasks into a role-playing game.
4. Evernote: A comprehensive note-taking and organizing tool for capturing ideas and plans.
5. Pomodoro: A time management tool using the Pomodoro Technique for increased productivity.

Online Courses and Workshops

1. Coursera: Courses on productivity, time management, and habit formation.
2. Udemy: Workshops on goal setting, self-discipline, and personal development.
3. Skillshare: Classes on creating productive habits and overcoming procrastination.
4. LinkedIn Learning: Modules on resilience, decision-making, and personal growth.
5. TED Talks: A vast collection of motivational talks and insights on productivity, resilience, and personal development.

These additional resources can further aid your journey toward personal and professional growth, providing tools, literature, and online courses to deepen your understanding and practice proactive habits while overcoming procrastination.

For your reference, some practical exercises and templates are added in the book's last pages. These will help you apply the concepts discussed throughout the book.

1. **Goal Setting Worksheet:** A structured template to define and set achievable short-term and long-term goals, complete with action steps and deadlines. (Refer Template 1)

2. **Procrastination Triggers Identification Exercise:** An exercise guiding you to identify their triggers for procrastination, encouraging self-reflection on the circumstances that lead to delays. (Refer Template 2)

3. **Daily Routine Planner:** A template to help you create a daily schedule that fosters productivity, allocating time blocks for tasks, breaks, and relaxation. (Refer Template 3)

4. **Decision-Making Matrix:** A tool to aid you in making more precise decisions by evaluating options based on urgency, importance, and long-term impact. (Refer Template 4)

5. **Resilience Building Journal Prompts:** Journaling prompts to encourage you to reflect on setbacks, challenges, and strategies employed to overcome them, fostering resilience. (Refer Template 5)

6. **Mindfulness and Focus Practice Exercises:** Simple mindfulness exercises and focus practices enhance concentration and reduce distractions, enabling better task engagement. (Refer Template 6)

7. **Proactive Habit Tracker:** A tracker for you to monitor the establishment of proactive habits, allowing them to note progress and reflect on consistency. (Refer Template 7)

These practical exercises and templates complement the book's content, enabling you to actively engage with the concepts discussed and apply them in your daily lives to conquer procrastination and embrace a proactive mindset.

10.1 TEMPLATE 1 - GOAL SETTING WORKSHEET

Goal

Title: [Write   your   goal   title   here]

_____

Goal Description: (Describe your goal in detail)

1. What specifically do you want to achieve?

   _____

   _____

   _____

   _____

   _____

   _____

2. Why is it important to you?

   _____

   _____

   _____

   _____

   _____

   _____

S.M.A.R.T. Goal Components

1. **Specific:** What exactly do you want to accomplish? Be as clear and specific as possible.

   _____

   _____

   _____

_____

_____

_____

2. **Measurable:** How will you know when you've achieved this goal? What metrics or indicators will you use?

_____

_____

_____

_____

_____

_____

3. **Achievable:** Given your current resources and constraints, is this goal realistic and attainable?

_____

_____

_____

_____

_____

_____

4. **Relevant:** Why is this goal important to you? How does it align with your values or long-term objectives?

_____

_____

_____

_____

_____

5. **Time-bound:** When do you plan to achieve this goal? Set a deadline for completion.

_____

_____

_____

_____

_____

_____

Action Steps: (Outline the specific actions you must take to achieve this goal. Break it down into smaller, manageable tasks or milestones.)

Serial No.	Task / Milestone	Date	Action Steps
1			
2			
3			
4			
5			

Resources Needed: (Identify any resources or support needed to accomplish these tasks.

(e.g., time, money, tools, skills, assistance).

1. _____

   _____

2. _____

   _____

3. _____

   _____

4. _____

   _____

5. _____

   _____

Progress Tracking: Keep track of your progress and adjust the plan as necessary.

This template provides a structured framework to effectively define, plan, and track your goals. You can create this template in a Word document or an Excel sheet, adding specific details tailored to your goals and aspirations.

10.2 TEMPLATE 2 - PROCRASTINATION TRIGGERS IDENTIFICATION EXERCISE

Step 1: Self-Reflection

(Think back to times when you've procrastinated. Identify specific instances and tasks where you were delaying or avoiding action.)

1. Task or Activity: [Describe the task or activity you procrastinated on]

_____

_____

_____

_____

2. Reason for Delay: [Identify the reasons or triggers for the delay]

_____

_____

_____

_____

3. Feelings or Emotions: [Note the emotions you experienced during the delay]

_____

_____

_____

_____

—

Step 2: Identifying Procrastination Triggers

(List common triggers or reasons for procrastination from the instances you have reflected on.)

Serial No.	Procrastination Trigger	Example	Feelings/Emotions
1	Fear of Failure	Not starting a task	Anxiety, Stress
2	Overwhelm	Multiple tasks	Frustration, Panic
3	Perfectionism	Polishing a Project	Inadequacy, Stress
4	Lack of Motivation	Starting a New Habit	Apathy, Disinterest
5	Distractions	Social Media, TV	Procrastination, Guilt

Step 3: Patterns and Analysis

Identify any patterns or recurring triggers from your examples. Reflect on the most common triggers and how they impact your behavior.

_____

_____

_____

_____

Step 4: Action Plan

Based on your identified triggers, plan strategies to manage or overcome these triggers in the future. Consider techniques like time-blocking, setting specific goals, or seeking support.)

_____

_____

_____

_____

_____

_____

_____

_____

This exercise helps you identify specific triggers that lead to procrastination. You can create this template in a Word document or an Excel sheet, entering the triggers and emotions you experience during procrastination to develop a deeper understanding and plan strategies for overcoming these triggers.

10.3 TEMPLATE 3 - DAILY ROUTINE PLANNER

Date: [Insert Date]

Morning Routine

Time	Activity
5:00 AM	Wakeup
6:00 AM	Exercise / Yoga / Morning Walk
7:00 AM	Breakfast and Daily News
8:00 AM	Commute / Travel to Work

Workday Schedule:

Time	Activity
9:00 AM	Work / Task 1
10:30 AM	Break / Stretch
11:00 AM	Work / Task 2
12:30 PM	Lunch and Relaxation
2:00 PM	Work / Task 3
3:30 PM	Break / Stretch
4:00 PM	Work / Task 4
5:00 PM	Review and Plan
6:00 PM	Commute / Travel to Home

Evening Routine

Time	Activity
7:00 PM	Exercise / Physical Activity

7:30 PM	Personal Projects / Development
8:00 PM	Dinner & Family Time
9:00 PM	Relaxation/Reading / TV

Night Routine

Time	Activity
9.30 PM	Wind-down / Meditation
10:00 PM	Journaling / Reflection
10.30 PM	Bedtime / Relaxation

You can personalize this template by adding specific activities, adjusting times, and incorporating their routines and tasks. This planner assists in organizing your daily schedule, promoting productivity, and balancing work, personal activities, and relaxation. You can create this template in a Word document or an Excel sheet for ease of use and modification.

10.4 TEMPLATE 4 - DECISION-MAKING MATRIX

Decision to be Made: [Insert Decision Topic]

_____

_____

_____

____

Factors to Consider

S. No	Factor	Option A	Option B	Option C
1	Urgency	High	Moderate	Low
2	Importance	Critical	Important but not urgent	Low Important
3	Long-Term Impact	Significant Impact	Moderate Impact	Minimal Impact
4	Resource Availability	Resources readily available	Moderate resources	Limited Resources
5	Personal Alignment	Aligned with personal goals	Partial alignment	Not aligned with goals

Evaluation

- **Weighting (1-5):** Assign a weight to each factor based on its relevance to the decision.
- **Score (1-5):** Rate each option on a scale based on the factor's significance for that option.

Overall Assessment

Option	Weighted (1 – 25)	Final Score (Average)
Option A		
Option B		
Option C		

Decision: [After evaluating, select the most suitable option based on the scores and overall assessment]

_____

_____

This template helps you analyze and compare multiple options by assessing various factors and assigning scores to make a well-informed decision. You can create this matrix in a Word document or an Excel sheet, customize it based on your decision criteria, and use it to evaluate different options methodically.

10.5 Template 5 - Resilience Building Journal Prompts

Prompt 1: Reflecting on Resilience

Reflect on a recent challenge or setback you faced.

- Describe the situation and your initial reactions.

  _____

  _____

  _____

  _____

  _____

- How did you cope with the situation?

  _____

  _____

  _____

  _____

- What strengths or skills did you draw upon?

  _____

  _____

  _____

  _____

  _____

Prompt 2: Turning Adversity into Opportunity

Think of a difficult situation that ultimately led to personal growth.

- What did you learn from this experience?

  _____

  _____

  _____

  _____

  _____

- How did you adapt or grow as a result?

  _____

  _____

  _____

  _____

  _____

- What strengths did you discover about yourself?

  _____

  _____

  _____

  _____

  _____

Prompt 3: Resilience Strategies

List at least three strategies you use to build resilience.

- How do these strategies help you during challenging times?

  _____

  _____

  _____

_____

_____

- Which strategy has been the most effective for you?

_____

_____

_____

_____

_____

- Are there new strategies you'd like to explore?

_____

_____

_____

_____

Prompt 4: Accepting Change and Uncertainty

Reflect on when you had to navigate a significant change or uncertainty.

- How did you manage this situation?

_____

_____

_____

_____

- What strategies did you use to find stability or acceptance?

_____

_____

_____

_____

_____

- What did you learn about yourself from this experience?

_____

_____

_____

_____

_____

Prompt 5: Seeking Support

Describe your support network during tough times.

- How do friends, family, or other resources assist in your resilience?

_____

_____

_____

_____

_____

- Do you have any strategies for seeking support when needed?

_____

_____

_____

_____

_____

Prompt 6: Planning for Future Challenges

Think about potential challenges that might arise in the future.

- How can you apply your resilience strategies to these scenarios?

  _____

  _____

  _____

  _____

  _____

- What proactive steps can you take to prepare for these challenges?

  _____

  _____

  _____

  _____

  _____

This journal prompt template encourages you to reflect on your experiences, resilience strategies, and personal growth. You can create this template in a Word document or an Excel sheet, use it for journaling, and adapt the questions to your specific situations to foster resilience and personal development.

10.6 TEMPLATE 6 - MINDFULNESS AND FOCUS PRACTICE EXERCISES

1. **Mindful Breathing:** Find a comfortable, quiet space. Sit or lie down, close your eyes, and focus on your breath. Inhale deeply for a count of 4, hold for 2, and exhale for 6. Repeat this for a few minutes, focusing on the sensation of your breath.

2. **Body Scan Meditation:** Lie down or sit comfortably. Start from your toes and gradually move upward, paying attention to each body part. Notice any tension or sensations without judgment, and consciously release the tension as you move through each body part.

3. **Mindful Eating:** Choose a small piece of food (like a raisin or nut). Examine it closely, noticing its texture, color, and shape. Take time to smell it, touch it, and slowly place it in your mouth. Chew slowly, focusing on the taste and texture.

4. **Focused Attention:** Pick a small object (a pen, a stone, or a flower). Please spend a few minutes examining it in detail. Concentrate on its features, texture, and shape. Try to notice details you might usually overlook.

5. **Guided Meditation:** Listen to a guided meditation or mindfulness session through apps or online resources. Follow the instructions, paying attention to the guidance provided.

6. **Mindful Walking**: Take a slow, deliberate walk. Focus on each step, the sensation of your feet touching the ground, and the movement of your body. Pay attention to your surroundings, noticing the sights, sounds, and sensations around you.

7. **Visualization Practice:** Sit comfortably and visualize a calming scene or a place you find peaceful. Picture the details – the colors, textures, and sensations. Engage all your senses in this mental exercise.

You can use these exercises to practice mindfulness and focus regularly, aiming to improve concentration, reduce stress, and increase awareness in daily life. You can incorporate these exercises into your daily routine or allocate specific time slots for practicing mindfulness.

10.7 TEMPLATE 7 - PROACTIVE HABIT TRACKER

Habit to Track: [Name]

Week Starting: [Insert Date]

Date	Habit Completed (Yes / No)	Notes / Comments
Date	Yes / No	Note progress or any observations

Notes:

- Use 'Y' for days the habit was completed and 'N' for days it was missed.
- In the Notes section, jot down observations, challenges faced, or any adjustments made during the habit-building process.

You can use this tracker to monitor your progress in cultivating proactive habits. You can customize the habit name and tracking period, then regularly fill in the table with 'Yes' or 'No' to indicate whether you completed the habit. Additionally, the Notes section allows you to record details or reflections about your progress and any challenges faced during the habit-building journey. This template can be created in a Word document or an Excel sheet for easy tracking and analysis.

Acknowledgments

In penning the contents of "Achieve It Now: Beat Procrastination for a Brighter Tomorrow," I am profoundly indebted to a constellation of guiding lights and steadfast supporters whose contributions and encouragement have illuminated the path to crafting this guide. Their unwavering support, insights, and inspiration have shaped the very essence of this work.

First and foremost, my heartfelt gratitude extends to all whose guidance and unflagging encouragement transformed the vision of this book into a reality. Your mentorship and belief in the importance of this message have been an invaluable compass, guiding each chapter's creation and molding the narrative within these pages.

I sincerely thank my family, whose unwavering support and understanding breathed life into these words. Your patience, feedback, and commitment to the vision of this book were invaluable in shaping its form and essence.

I thank the diligent editorial team and the publishing house, whose expertise and dedication helped shape this manuscript into its final form. Your commitment to refining the message and ensuring its clarity has been instrumental in bringing this work to fruition.

Lastly, I sincerely thank the readers who have chosen "Achieve It Now" as companions in their journey to conquer procrastination. Your choice to delve into these pages signifies a commitment to self-improvement and personal growth. I'm profoundly grateful for your trust in this work. I hope it provides the tools and insights necessary to navigate the labyrinth of procrastination and emerge triumphant on the path to a brighter future.

To all those who have contributed, directly or indirectly, to the realization of this project, your support and belief have been invaluable. Thank you for being part of this journey toward conquering procrastination and embracing a future teeming with realized aspirations and boundless potential.

ABOUT THE AUTHOR

 The author has an impressive professional background of over three decades in private and government IT. Ayurvedic life management and yoga instructor certifications are also his. Active Toastmasters member.

He was born in Pulgaon, a peaceful village in Wardha, Maharashtra, on August 26, 1968. He graduated from Madhya Pradesh's Ordinance Factory Higher Secondary School Katni in 1984 in Hindi. He earned an engineering degree from Government Engineering College Jabalpur in 1990 and a part-time MBA in 2010. The author lives in Nagpur, also known as Orange City, and enjoys listening to music, watching movies, reading motivational literature, traveling, and volunteering.

He believes that challenges are opportunities and that success requires perseverance.

Stay connected and inspired by following him on Facebook, LinkedIn, and Instagram.

https://www.facebook.com/dilip.patil.3979

https://www.linkedin.com/in/dilip-patil-4066a518

https://www.instagram.com/dilip.patil.3979

DISCOVER MORE OF OUR TITLES

Beyond the pages of 'Achieve It Now: Beat Procrastination for a Brighter Tomorrow,' I'm thrilled to introduce a series of my other literary creations, available in both e-book and paperback formats across various platforms. Each offering is a valuable companion on your personal and professional development journey.

1. Empowering Yourself to Achieve Success: Delve into the core principles of personal development, guided by transformative mindset shifts, actionable strategies, and inspiring anecdotes.

2. The Path to Lasting Happiness: Explore the keys to enduring happiness, including purpose, mindset, relationships, resilience, and more. Master communication finesse, cultivate empathy, and acquire skills leading to multifaceted success.

3. Yoga Flow for Tech Minds: Enhance productivity, reduce stress, and foster holistic well-being in the digital age with practices harmonizing ancient wisdom and modern science.

4. The Success Habits: Instill winning habits and unlock your full potential by delving into the psychology of success. Equip yourself with actionable strategies to elevate your productivity, career, and fulfillment.

5. The Success Mindset: Uncover the secrets to goal attainment and crafting your desired reality. Learn how to nurture a winning mindset, dismantle limiting beliefs, and unleash boundless potential.

6. Endurance: Delve deep into enduring and transcending life's tests—a valuable companion on your journey of growth and adaptability.

7. The Power of Adaptability: Complementing 'The Success Formula,' this book explores the remarkable influence of adaptability in shaping destinies.

8. The Success Formula: Discover the art of success and unleash your potential with fundamental principles, practical tools, and real-life stories. Explore the guide to personal and professional excellence.

9. Discover the Power of Gratitude: This book is about gratitude and its transformative power to help you grow personally and professionally.

These diverse works provide insights, strategies, and wisdom to help you excel. They inspire and guide you toward personal growth, career success, and well-being. Transformative content from these books is available on [mention platforms], complementing your personal and professional journey.

YOUR FEEDBACK MATTERS

"Your feedback is the compass that guides the improvement journey."

Dear Readers,

I hope you found 'Achieve It Now: Beat Procrastination for a Brighter Tomorrow' enlightening and transformative. Your insights are invaluable, and I invite you to share your thoughts with me.

Your Feedback!

1. What resonated with you the most in this book?

2. Were the strategies effective in addressing your procrastination challenges?

3. How has applying the principles impacted your personal and professional life?

4. Do you have any suggestions for improvement or topics you'd like covered in future works?

Your feedback will not only help enhance this book but also contribute to the creation of content that addresses your specific needs.

Connect with Me

I am eager to hear from you! Feel free to share your thoughts via email at patildilip23@gmail.com, dilip.patil@patildilip.com, or on social media. Let's continue this journey of growth together.

Thank you for joining the 'Achieve It Now' community!

Warm regards,

Dilip Patil
Author, 'Achieve It Now: Beat Procrastination for a Brighter Tomorrow'

EXCITING NEWS AHEAD!

"The journey doesn't end here; it evolves."

I am thrilled to share a glimpse into the exciting future of the 'Procrastination Triumph Series.' Your overwhelming support for 'Achieve It Now: Beat Procrastination for a Brighter Tomorrow' has been truly inspiring. As we celebrate this milestone, I'm delighted to announce upcoming additions to the series that will further empower you on your personal and professional growth journey.

Stay Tuned for More Transformative Works!

Under the 'Procrastination Triumph Series banner,' I am diligently crafting new volumes that delve deeper into the intricacies of conquering procrastination. Each book is designed to be a beacon of guidance, offering insights, strategies, and practical wisdom to navigate the complexities of life.

Join the Community

Be part of this transformative community, where we explore the art of overcoming procrastination and unlocking untapped potential. Your continued support and engagement fuel creating content tailored to your needs.

Get Ready for the Next Book

As we embark on this exciting journey together, anticipate a series of powerful tools, insights, and strategies to enhance your personal and professional life.

"The journey of a thousand miles begins with a single step. Embrace the path of continuous improvement."

Thank you for being integral to the 'Procrastination Triumph Series community. Together, let's explore new horizons and conquer the challenges.

Warm regards,

DILIP PATIL
Author, 'Achieve It Now: Beat Procrastination for a Brighter Tomorrow'

Your Free Gift

"In gratitude for your support and commitment to personal growth."

Click the link or scan the QR code below to download your gift.

"The Success Formula: Achieve Personal Growth, Excel Professionally, Unlock Your Potential, Transform Your Life."

www.ingramcontent.com/pod-product-compliance
Lightning Source LLC
Chambersburg PA
CBHW062332290526
45794CB00005B/2003